GUIDE TO
GREECE

MICHAEL MARCH

Consultant: Loty Petrovits-Andrutsopulou

Highlights for Children

CONTENTS

On the cover: The Parthenon is a huge temple, now in ruins, which was built more than 2,000 years ago. It forms part of the Acropolis, the protected part of the ancient city of Athens, the capital of Greece.

The publisher is grateful for the guidance of the Greece National Tourist Office in London, England, and to Loty Petrovits-Andrutsopulou of Athens, Greece. Loty Petrovits-Andrutspulou is a writer, translator, lecturer, critic, former member of the executive committee of the International Board on Books for Young People (IBBY), associate editor of its international journal, *Bookbird,* and president of IBBY Greece.

Published by Highlights for Children
© 1999 Highlights for Children, Inc.
P.O. Box 18201
Columbus, Ohio 43218-0201
For information on *Top Secret Adventures,* visit
www.tsadventures.com or call 1-800-962-3661.

10 9
ISBN 0-87534-571-9

NORTH AMERICA

Tropic of Cancer

Equator

SOUTH AMERICA

Tropic of Capricorn

EUROPE

Greece

ASIA

AFRICA

AUSTRALIA

ANTARCTICA

△ **Greek flag** Blue and white are Greece's seafaring colors. The white cross represents the Greek Orthodox Church. The design was chosen after the Greek War of Independence against the Turks between 1821 and 1830.

GREECE AT A GLANCE

Area 50,949 square miles
  (131,957 km^2)
Population 10,688,058
Capital Athens, population 3,247,000
Other big cities Thessaloníki
  (356,449) Piraeus (172,025),
  Pátra (164,968)
Highest mountain Mount Olympus,
  9,570 feet (2,917 m)
Longest river Aliákmon, 185 miles
  (297 km)
Largest lake Megali Prespa,
  390 square miles (1,000 km^2)
  shared with Former Yugoslav
  Republic of Macedonia (FYROM),
  and Albania; 15 square miles
  (38 km^2) in Greece
Official language Greek

▽ **Greek stamps** The designs below show traditional Greek costumes as well as cultural artifacts and historic sites.

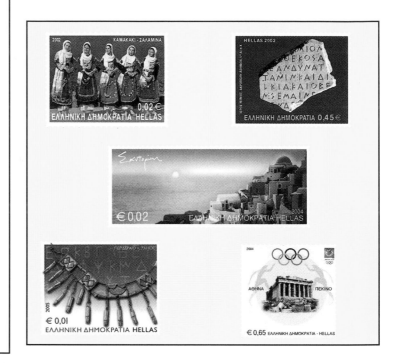

◁ **Greek money** The currency of Greece is the euro (€). The country belongs to the European Union (EU) and has the same currency as other EU member countries. For example, this note could be used in France or Ireland.

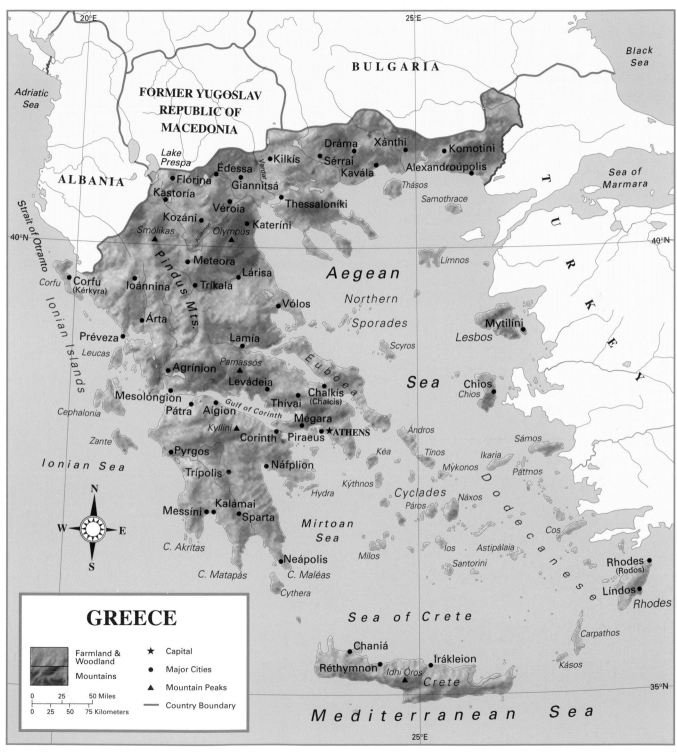

Black Sea

BULGARIA

Adriatic Sea

FORMER YUGOSLAV REPUBLIC OF MACEDONIA

ALBANIA

Lake Prespa

Dráma
Xánthi
Komotini
Sérrai
Alexandroúpolis
Kilkís
Kaválla
Édessa
Flórina
Kastoría
Giannitsá
Véroia
Thessaloníki
Kozáni
Kateríni
Smólikas ▲
Aliákmon
Olympus ▲

Sea of Marmara

Thásos
Samothrace

T
U
R
K
E
Y

40°N
40°N

Meteora
Lárisa
Ioánnina
Tríkala
Árta

Aegean

Límnos

Vólos

Northern
Sporades

Préveza

Lamía

Scyros

Sea

Lesbos

Mytilíni

Leucas

Agrínion
Parnassós ▲
Levádeia

Euboea

Chalkís
(Chalcis)
Thívai

Chios
Chios

Pindus Mts.

Ionian Islands

Corfu
(Kérkyra)
Corfu

Mesolóngion
Pátra
Aígion
Gulf of Corinth
Kyllíni ▲
Corinth
Mégara
Piraeus
★ATHENS

Strait of Otranto

Cephalonia

Zante

Pyrgós

Náfplion

Trípolis

Ándros
Kéa
Tínos
Sámos
Mýkonos
Ikaria
Pátmos

D
o
d
e
c
a
n
e
s
e

Ionian Sea

Messíni
Kalámai
Sparta

Mirtoan Sea

Kýthnos
Hydra

Cyclades
Páros
Náxos

Cos

Rhodes
(Rodos)

C. Akrítas

Neápolis

Mílos
Íos
Astipálaia

Líndos

C. Matapás
C. Maléas
Cythera

Santorini

Rhodes

Carpathos

Sea of Crete

Kásos

Chaniá

Réthymnon
Idhi Óros ▲
Irákleion

Crete

35°N

Mediterranean Sea

GREECE

Farmland & Woodland

Mountains

★ Capital
● Major Cities
▲ Mountain Peaks
— Country Boundary

0   25   50 Miles
0 25 50 75 Kilometers

N
W   E
S

BIRTHPLACE OF THE WESTERN WORLD

Greece is a beautiful ancient country in southeast Europe. Its borders stretch from the Balkan Peninsula out into the Mediterranean Sea across chains of islands.

In winter, the mountains are covered with snow. During the warm summers, millions of visitors from all over the world come to the lovely islands. Wildflowers in white, pink, and orange carpet the hillsides in spring and fall.

All over Greece you will see olive trees. People have been making olive oil here for thousands of years. In the north, the forests are home to the brown bear, gray wolf, lynx, boar, and other animals that are now rare elsewhere in Europe. From the tiny wagtail to the giant black vulture, millions of birds visit or live in Greece.

About 2,500 years ago, Greece was an important center of culture and learning. Greek ideas on art, medicine, technology, architecture, and government spread across Europe and beyond. The ancient Greeks were the first people to practice democracy.

▽ **Feast of Saint John** Women in traditional dress dance and celebrate this feast in Olymbos on Karpathos Island.

△ **Sunshine, sand, and sea** All over Greece, you will find beautiful beaches, where you can relax in the sun and where the water is warm for swimming.

▷ **Mountains and coast** On most of the Greek islands, as here on Hydra, towns and villages dot the coast. These rugged mountains fill the island's interior.

Nowadays, most countries in the Western Hemisphere are democracies. In fact, the word *democracy*, meaning "government by the people," comes from the Greek language.

All over Greece, you will find ruins of fine temples and palaces built long ago. In some of the more remote regions, you will also come across villages where little seems to have changed over the past 500 years.

The Greek people feel strongly about their traditions and customs. They have their own language and their own alphabet.

The majority of Greeks are Christians and are members of the Greek Orthodox Church. Music, dancing, and being friendly to strangers are major parts of the Greek way of life. Someone will nearly always greet you with a cheerful *"Kalee mé-ra"* ("Good morning") as you travel around Greece's small towns and villages.

CITY OF WISDOM

Athens is an ancient city surrounded by mountains and the sea. Since the last century, soon after the Greek people won their freedom from the Turks, Athens became the capital.

The modern city of Athens is home to more than three million people. It is by far the largest Greek city. Downtown Athens is full of cars, street vendors, outdoor markets, and historic sites. At one of the city's busiest road intersections stands the Arch of Hadrian. Built by the Romans in A.D. 132, its white marble is now gray with age.

On a nearby hill, you can see the famous ruins of the Acropolis. This area was the high, protected part of the city in ancient times. It is visible from all over Athens. Here, you can explore the remains of marble temples and statues that are more than 2,500 years old.

A magnificent huge marble building with tall columns stands above all the others. It is called the Parthenon, and it was built to house a giant statue of Athena, the Greek goddess of wisdom. The city of Athens is named for Athena.

Nearby, you will find two semicircular open-air theaters with stone seats. The larger one, the Theater of Dionysos, is the birthplace of Greek tragedy and was the first theater built of stone. The smaller one, the Theater of Herodes Atticus, has been completely restored. On summer evenings, you can sit and watch Greek plays here.

Below the Acropolis is Athens's bustling Plaka district, where the small old town of Athens was located during the Turkish occupation. Its maze of narrow streets are crammed with *tavernas* (Greek restaurants) and shops. You can enjoy *moussaka* (minced meat, eggplant, and thick white cream) or the favorite local dish, *patsas* (tripe soup).

◁ **Shops in the Plaka district** Here, you can buy leather goods, real sponges, carpets, and even your own *bouzouki*, a Greek-style mandolin, as souvenirs.

▷ **Lunchtime, Greek–style** Here is a delicious assortment of *souvlaki* (skewered meat), salad made with tomatoes, olives, and feta (soft, white) cheese, chilies, bread, taramasaláta (smoked fish roe), and dolmádes (stuffed vine leaves).

▽ **Tomb of the Unknown Soldier, Athens** Greek guards parade in front of the monument that honors unidentified heroes killed in past wars.

FROM THE MARKETPLACE TO MARATHON

In ancient Athens, the Agora was the marketplace. It was also the meeting place for Greek thinkers. The great philosopher Socrates used to win lively debates with his opponents here. Much later, Saint Paul arrived to preach the Christian message.

A short subway ride will take you near the National Archaeological Museum. One of the finest of its many treasures is the Death Mask of Agamémnon. It was cast in gold from a mold of a dead king's face more than 3,000 years ago. Despite its name, the face is not that of Agamémnon, but that of an earlier king who died 300 years before him.

▽**Athens as seen from Lykavittos Hill** From a height of 745 feet (227 m), there are some stunning views of the city and out to sea.

△ **Getting around on Hydra** Donkeys are the only way to travel around Hydra. No motorized vehicles are allowed on the island.

◁ **Bathing in Poros** The island of Poros is famous for its sandy bays and clear waters. Many Athenians like to spend the weekend on the island.

Piraeus is a big, busy town at the southern end of Athens's subway line. Piraeus is as old as Athens and is the country's main international seaport. Ferries depart from here heading for Aegina and most of the other Greek islands. Aegina was once, very briefly, Greece's capital. Today it is best known for its pistachio nuts.

From Piraeus, you can follow the coast road to Cape Soúnion. Here, high on a cliff top, the gleaming, white marble Temple of Poseidon looks out to sea. Poseidon was the ancient Greeks' god of the sea.

Farther north, one of Greece's most-famous battles took place. In 490 B.C., the Greeks defeated the Persians on the plain at Marathon. A messenger ran the 26.2 miles (42 km) back to Athens to spread the news. Still today, that is the distance of marathon races held around the world.

WARS AND GAMES

Buses and trains going from Athens to Corinth cross the spectacular, high-walled Corinth Canal. This region of Greece, on the southern side of the canal, is called the Peloponnese.

Just outside the modern town of Corinth, you can explore the site of ancient Corinth. Here, you will find fascinating Greek and Roman ruins spread over a wide area. Corinth, at its height, was Athens's great rival. The two cities even went to war with each other.

Long before then, the kingdom of Mycenae to the south was all powerful. The poet Homer wrote how King Agamémnon of Mycenae led the armies of Greece against Troy in Asia (now in Turkey). Ancient Mycenae lies in the bare foothills of two mountains. You can wander through the remains of Agamémnon's once-splendid palace, and visit the *tholos* (beehive-shaped tomb) where he is buried.

The lovely old port of Náfplion is an hour's bus ride away from Corinth. Náfplion was once a stronghold of the Venetians, people who came from the city of Venice in Italy. The Venetians built many of the houses and narrow streets that you see in Náfplion's Old Town. Bourtzi was one of three fortresses built to defend the town. It stands on a tiny island, which can be reached only by boat.

Sparta is a small town in the southern Peloponnese. It is nestled in a valley beneath snow-capped mountains. Some 2,400 years ago, Sparta was a kingdom whose mighty army won two wars against the kingdom of Athens. At the west side of the Peloponnese, where the ancient holy area of Olympia was, you can see the huge stadium where the first Olympic Games were held nearly 3,000 years ago.

The Olympic Games were held every four years. Even when at war, places such as Sparta and Athens would call a truce and take part in the games.

△ **The Corinth Canal** The canal opened to shipping in 1893. It is 3.5 miles (6 km) long and 75 feet (23 m) wide. The sides rise almost vertically 295 feet (90 m) above the water.

△ **Olive harvest in the Peloponnese** Greek people have always valued their olive trees. In the past, whole forests were cleared to make fields for planting them.

◁ **Theater at Epidaurus, near Náfplion** The ancient theater seats 14,000 people. If you drop a coin in the middle, the sound can be heard at the back seats.

THE WESTERN ISLANDS

The Ionian islands are a string of islands off Greece's west coast that stretch from the Peloponnese to the country's border with Albania. Here, mountains and forests overlook sandy beaches and glistening water. Oak and maple trees grow alongside orchids, acacias, and eucalyptus trees.

Cephalonia, to the north, is the biggest of the Ionian islands. It is rugged, with high mountains and underground caves. The female of the rare loggerhead turtle lays eggs on the southern shores. Zante Island lies off the Peloponnesian coast. Since ancient times, this island has been praised for its beauty and its emerald-green seas.

The island of Leucas was once part of mainland Greece. Then, in the eighth century B.C., the Corinthians dug a canal, opening the tiny neck of land that connected Leucas to the mainland. If you walk through the town of Lefkás, you will see houses with upper stories made of corrugated iron. These houses are built to withstand earthquake shocks, which do occur from time to time. Vasilikí Bay, in the southern part of the island, is one of Europe's best spots for windsurfing.

Corfu is the Ionian island that is farthest north. It is also the greenest. Corfu is very popular with tourists. In the mountains, the air is scented with basil, rosemary, thyme, oregano, and other herbs that grow here. The Greeks use herbs not only in their cooking, but also as medicine.

The international ferry that sails from Italy to Pátra, capital of the Peloponnese region, stops at Corfu. You can then take a train from Pátra to Diakoptón, a pretty village with lemon groves. Here, you can board another train for the thrilling journey to Kalávryta through the steep Vouraïkós Gorge. The train crosses bridges, goes through tunnels, and speeds along overhanging ledges.

▷**Journey through Vouraïkós Gorge**
The train climbs 2,300 feet (700 m) over a distance of 14 miles (22.5 km). The journey from Diakoptón to Kalávryta takes one hour, stopping once.

▽**Passengers arriving at Corfu Harbor**
Ferries cross between here and the island of Paxoí; the town of Igoumenítsa, on the Greek mainland; and the town of Brindisi in Italy.

△ **Paleokastritsa, on Corfu** The popular resort on the west coast of the island has beautiful sand and pebble beaches overlooked by lush green hills.

HEROES AND PROPHETS

Mesolóngion is a small town on the shores of a lagoon, north of the Gulf of Pátra. In 1824, the English poet George Byron came here to help the Greeks fight for their freedom from the Turks. Soon afterward, he became ill and died. Although his body was returned to England, his heart is buried in the town's cemetery for heroes. A marble statue of the poet stands over the spot.

The Sanctuary of Apollo at Delphi, near Levádeia, is a much older monument. Its ruins stand on the slopes of Mount Parnassós. Apollo was the ancient Greek god of prophecy. For centuries, people came here to ask the priestess, or oracle, questions about the future. On most occasions, the answers they received puzzled them.

Farther east, a bridge spans the Evripos Channel between the Greek mainland and the island of Euboea. Amazingly, the tide in this narrow channel changes seven times a day, instead of twice, as in most other places. This activity of nature baffled even Aristotle, one of the greatest thinkers in ancient Greece.

Nearby is Skyros, one of the Sporades Islands. The waters around these islands are home to the rare Mediterranean monk seal. Ferries to and from the Sporades dock at the lush, green Pelion Peninsula. Here, you will find mountain villages with whitewashed, half-timbered houses, and you can enjoy a hearty bean soup, the favorite local dish.

On Skyros, many older men still wear traditional baggy pants, and people decorate their homes with copper plates and hand-carved furniture. Skyros was once famous throughout Greece for its goat's milk. Every year, for two Sundays in spring, the men put on goat masks and the women dress up for the island's traditional goat festival.

▷ **The Temple of Apollo, Delphi** This was the main building of the sanctuary. In the fourth century B.C., a priestess, or oracle, answered pilgrims' questions to the god Apollo.

16

◁ **Meteora, in Central Greece** Since the Middle Ages some 500 years ago, Christian monks have found peace in the quiet monasteries built among the rocky pinnacles of Meteora.

▽ **Women in black, a common sight in Greece's countryside** Traditionally, when a Greek man dies, his widow must wear black for a few years afterward.

MOUNTAINS AND GODS

The mountain villages of northern Greece are famous for traditional, woolen *flokati* rugs. People have been making them in the same way for hundreds of years. First, they weave the rugs loosely. Then they leave them under rushing water to shrink and tighten the twisted wool pile.

Ioánnina, the capital of the Epirus region, is a good place to buy a *flokati* rug. This town is an interesting mix of old and new. The two mosques, Muslim places of worship, inside the old city walls were built by the Turks in the eighteenth century.

Ioánnina is the "gateway" to Vikos-Aoös National Park. Here, in the mountains, bears, wolves, and wild boar roam the forests of maple, oak, and fir trees. Here, too, you will find pretty villages with houses' roofs made of slate dug from the mountains.

Every day, planes fly from Ioánnina to Thessaloníki. This is Greece's second-largest city and the capital of the Macedonia region. More than 2,000 years ago, the Macedonian king Alexander the Great established a huge Greek empire. You can visit Alexander's birthplace at Pella, outside Thessaloníki.

▷ **Brown bear** Small numbers of brown bears live in the mountains of northern Greece. Like the gray wolf, which also has its home here, the brown bear is now quite rare.

◁ **Mount Olympus, Greece's highest mountain** The tallest peak reaches 9,570 feet (2,917 m). The ancient Greeks believed that this mountain was the home of the gods.

△ **The White Tower in Thessaloníki** The tower was built in the 15th century and was later used as a prison. Today, it is a museum.

Before setting off to conquer new lands in Syria, Palestine, Egypt, and Mesopotamia, Alexander the Great made sacrifices to the gods at the foot of Mount Olympus. Today, you can follow marked trails to the famous mountain's summit. It takes two days to get there, staying overnight at a mountain camp. You need sunscreen, a sturdy pair of walking boots, and a parka to keep out the wet and cold, even in summer.

Near Greece's northwestern border, you will discover a wonderland of lakes and lakeside villages. On the eastern frontier, you can see wetlands that are regularly visited by hundreds of thousands of migrating birds.

THE NORTH AEGEAN ISLANDS

Samothrace is a small island in the North Aegean Sea. The famous statue of the Greek goddess of victory, Nike, came from this island. Called *Winged Victory*, the statue now stands in the Louvre Museum in Paris, France. Here, in a valley beneath Mount Sáos, you can visit the ruins of the Sanctuary of the Great Gods, where Nike once stood.

The biggest of the North Aegean Islands is Lesbos. Around 90,000 people live here. Lesbos produces some of Greece's finest olive oil. Olives are grown all over the southern and eastern parts of the island, and you will see many olive-oil refineries. The western part of Lesbos is rocky and bare, like the surface of the Moon. On the west coast, you will find a petrified forest—trees that have turned to stone over millions of years.

There is one ferry a day from Lesbos to the island of Chios. In the southern part of Chios, you will find pretty, medieval villages with narrow streets crossed by archways.

△ **A Kentish plover nesting on the sands of Lesbos** Some 280 species of birds live on the island or rest here during their migrations from Africa to northern Europe.

▷**A Greek Orthodox priest in the village of Pyrgi, on Chios** The houses and the church on the village square are decorated with black sand and white lime.

For centuries, the villagers here have made their living from the mastic trees growing on the surrounding hills. Mastic gum was used both as medicine and as chewing gum. In the local stores you can buy some mastic chewing gum as a souvenir.

Farther south is Sámos, a green island where the mountain air smells of the jasmine flower. People here grow white grapes for making sweet wine, and they grow orchids to sell abroad. The well-known mathematician Pythagoras was born on Sámos. His name lives on in Pythagorio, a resort on the island's southeastern coast. Pythagorio stands on the site of the great, ancient city of Sámos. You can explore the tunnel that once brought water to the city from the mountains. The tunnel was built more than 2,500 years ago.

▽ **The hills above Kokkari, on Sámos**
Breathing in mountain air while looking down to the sea on Sámos makes hiking a pleasure.

THE SUNKEN ISLAND

The Cyclades Islands form a cluster in the south Aegean Sea, part of the Mediterranean Sea. At the height of summer, a cooling wind blows across the islands and coasts of eastern Greece. It is called the *meltemi*.

The Cyclades are everything you might imagine a Greek island to be. Whitewashed buildings in bright sunshine stand out against the clear blue sky. Sheep and goats graze on the rocky hillsides. Blue-green seas wash onto sandy beaches.

Páros Island is part of the Cyclades. Since early times, this island has been known for its pure-white marble. You can see this marble in the columns of the beautiful church of Ekatontaplyiani, which stands near the harbor. From here, you can catch a ferry to most of the other main islands in the Cyclades.

On Mýkonos Island, there are shops selling the latest fashions. The houses have brightly colored balconies, with purple and orange flowers called bougainvilleas growing against the white walls. Off the west coast of Mýkonos is the tiny island of Delos. The Theater of Delos was built 2,300 years ago. Here, among the ruins of the theater and ancient houses, you will discover some lovely old mosaics—pictures made from small pieces of tile or stone.

The island of Santoríni, or Thíra, is known as the sunken island. It curves around a huge sunken crater. In about 1500 B.C., a volcano erupted with such force that the center of the island collapsed into the sea. In the southern part of the island, you can visit the ancient site of Akrotiri. This was a thriving town before it was buried under the volcanic ash. Archaeologists are now uncovering the ruins. They have found some well-preserved, three-story buildings.

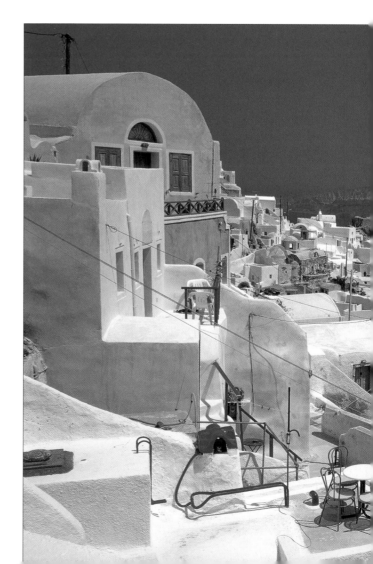

▷**Walking on Thíra** The volcanic lava and pumice, a light volcanic rock, in the hills range in color from deep-pink to black. The beaches consist of dark pebbles or black sand.

▽ **A church on the cliff top at Santorini** From up high, there are spectacular views of the sea and the rocks below.

△ **The windmills of Mýkonos** More tourists visit Mýkonos than any other Greek island. The windmills—seen here in the distance—are in the Little Venice area, near the waterfront.

THE STATUE AND THE SAINT

On a map, the Dodecanese Islands speckle the Aegean Sea, near the southwest coast of Turkey. These islands, far from the Greek mainland, have been invaded many times. In fact, they were given back to Greece by Italy in 1947.

Rhodes is by far the biggest island in the Dodecanese. It gets 300 days of sunshine a year. Long ago, the people of Rhodes built a huge bronze statue in honor of Helios-Apollo, also the god of sunlight. (*Helios* is the Greek word for *sun*.) It stood 100 feet (31 m) high and towered over Mandraki Harbor in the city of Rhodes, the island's capital. The statue became known as the *Colossus of Rhodes*, and was one of the Seven Wonders of the Ancient World. Today, two much smaller bronze statues of deer, one of a doe, the other of a stag, mark the place where the Colossus probably stood.

◁ **Sponge seller on Rhodes** Sponges are the skeletons of jellylike animals that live in the sea. They are collected, then bleached.

▷ **The narrow streets of Líndos, Rhodes** Tourists ride donkeys to the center of the hilltop village.

▷ **Grand Master's Palace, city of Rhodes** In the Middle Ages, the Grand Master was in charge of the Knights of St. John. This was his home. Today it is a museum.

In the center of the modern city of Rhodes is the medieval town. Here, you can explore the high walls built by the Knights of St. John, a religious and military order who ruled the island for more than 200 years. You can walk down the cobblestone Avenue of the Knights where they lived.

One thousand years ago, St. John himself lived in exile on Pátmos Island, to the north of Rhodes. A huge, gray-walled monastery dedicated to him stands on the island. Olympos Village, on the island of Carpathos, is a living museum. Here, the women wear traditional goatskin boots and brightly colored long embroidered skirts, waistcoats, and scarves.

Carpathos Island, to the southwest of Rhodes, has a long tradition of sponge fishing. When the divers pick the sponges off the seabed, the sponges are black. You can visit the island's factory where the sponges are bleached pale-yellow and made ready for sale to be used in cleaning and bathing.

BETWEEN TWO CONTINENTS

Crete is an island of great natural beauty, with mountains, beaches, and forests of palm trees. It lies between Europe and Africa and is the largest of the Greek islands. Here, people still sing their soulful, traditional songs and dance their fiery dances. You will see men in loose black pants called breeches. They also wear the Cretan fringed kerchiefs, or scarves.

On the north coast is the bustling city of Irákleion, or Candia, the island's capital.

In 1541, one of the world's greatest painters was born here. He later went to Spain and became known as El Greco, which is Spanish for "the Greek." A marble bust of the painter stands in the center of the city, in a square named for him.

Outside Irakleion, you can visit Knossós, the ancient capital of Crete. Here, you can explore a magnificent palace that has been reconstructed to look as it did over 3,500 years ago. Some of the colorful frescoes are now in Irákleion's archaeological museum. Frescoes are scenes painted directly on walls that have been spread with wet plaster. One very famous fresco from Knossós shows a young man somersaulting over a bull.

From Chaniá, Crete's second-largest city, you can head inland toward the spectacular Samariá Gorge. To trek through the gorge takes about six hours. Along the way, you will see millions of wildflowers. The rare wild Cretan goat, the kri-kri, lives here. At the start, the gorge is wide and gaping, but later, the walls close in until they are only 10 feet (3 m) apart. On the other side of the great gorge, you will find a welcoming beach. Now that your travels through Greece are complete, you can relax and cool off here.

◁ **The Palace of Knossós** Archaeologists have restored much of this ancient site, like these two wallpaintings, called frescoes, that show servants carrying jars.

◁ **Trekking through Samariá Gorge** The gorge begins just below Omalós Plateau. It is 11 miles (18 km) long, and its vertical walls rise to 1,640 feet (500 m).

▽ **Venetian houses on Crete** Both Chaniá and Réthymnon, towns in the western part of the island, have a lovely old Venetian section overlooking the harbor.

GREECE FACTS AND FIGURES

People

People who were born in Greece make up nearly all of its population. They are partly descended from ancient Greeks, but have mixed heritage. There is a small Muslim population, as well as many temporary workers and refugees from Albania, who entered Greece in the 1990s.

Trade and Industry

Factories in Greece produce a wide range of goods, including canned fruit and vegetables, cloth, shoes and leather goods, paper, chemicals, rubber, plastics, cement, and electrical machinery. Most factories and industrial plants are located around Athens and Thessaloníki.

There is some mining in Greece. Lignite (a soft coal), bauxite (for making aluminum), and both white and colored marble are taken from the earth.

Tourism and shipping are the most important industries. About 14 million tourists visit Greece each year. Greek-owned ships,

△ **Fruit Seller on Corfu** Greece's sunny climate is ideal for growing oranges, lemons, and melons, as well as apples and cherries.

along with ships registered in Greece, make up the world's largest merchant fleet. Among the major ports are Piraeus, Pátra, and Thessaloníki.

Farming

Today, farming is less important to Greece than is industry. Less than 25% of the people work on the land. Only about a quarter of the land is used for growing crops. Farmers grow wheat, barley, corn, rice, sugar beets, tobacco, cotton, tomatoes, grapes, potatoes, olives, oranges, and other fruit and vegetables. Olives and olive oil, tobacco, and grapes and wine are sold to other countries.

Much more land is used as grazing land than is cultivated. Sheep and goats are raised throughout the country. They outnumber cattle by more than twenty to one. These animals provide meat, cheese, and milk as well as wool and leather. Chickens are also raised for eggs and meat.

Fishing

The fishing industry is very small. Out of a total 10.5 million Greeks, only 20,000 of them fish for a living. All kinds of fish are caught—cod, swordfish, sole, snapper, red mullet, sardines, whitebait, squid and octopus, as well as mussels, shrimp, lobster, and crawfish. Sponges are also gathered off the seabed. Greece's few rivers provide some trout, carp, and other freshwater fish.

Food

Every region of Greece has its own special dishes. For example, Ándros in the Cyclades is famous for its *froutaliá*, a spearmint-flavored potato-and-sausage omelet. Here are some dishes that are popular everywhere:

Mezédes: Appetizers that include dips, such as *tzatzíki* (garlic-flavored cucumber and yogurt) and *taramasaláta* (smoked fish roe), as well as *feta* cheese (white sheep's-milk cheese), olives, *dolmádes* (stuffed vine leaves), and *mavromátika* (black-eyed peas). *Soutzoutkákia* is spicy lamb or beef sausages cooked in a tomato sauce and served with rice and salad.

Schools

All schooling, from preschool through university, is free. There are, however, many private schools, especially at the primary level. Children start primary school at age 6. At 12, they enter high school, which is divided into the 3-year *gymnasio* and the 3-year *lýkeio*. At age 18, those with good grades go on to the universities.

△ **The front of a small village church**
In most Greek villages, the church is the focus of the community. At a Greek church wedding, family, villagers, and visitors are welcomed.

The Media

There are fifteen national newspapers published in Greek. They are all widely read. *Athens News* is in English and appears every day except Mondays. It carries world news as well as Greek news. *Atlantis* is a monthly magazine in English and includes articles on politics and travel.

Greek television viewers can choose from twelve regular channels, and some that are pay-per-view. There are two national radio stations, and many local radio stations are starting up, especially around Athens.

Music and Dance

Each region of Greece has its own folk dances. But the *kalamatianós* is performed everywhere. Originally, the dance came from the town of Kalamáta, in the Peloponnese. The dancers form a circle, holding each other's hands.

Literature and Drama

One of the greatest Greek writers was Homer. It is believed that he lived in the eighth century B.C., but his *Odyssey* and *Iliad* are still read today.

Some of the world's greatest plays were written in ancient Greece. Many are still performed.

GREECE FACTS AND FIGURES

Art and Architecture

The architecture of ancient Greece formed the basis of European architecture. The ancient Greeks developed the V-shaped roof and perfected the design of columns to support the roof.

Many ancient Greek marble statues, such as the *Venus de Milo*, are famous for their beauty. So too are ancient Greek vases. The well-known red-clay pottery with black figures was first made in Corinth over 2,500 years ago. The ancient Greeks also made beautiful jewelry.

Religion

About 98% of Greeks are Christians, belonging to the Greek Orthodox Church. Muslims make up 1% of the population, and the other 1% are Jews, Protestants, and Roman Catholics.

Festivals

Greeks really enjoy their festivals, and there are many to celebrate. Here are just a few of them:

△ **Children in national costume on Independence Day** The celebrations honor the start of Greece's War of Independence against the Turks.

March 25 **Independence Day**
April 23 **Agios Georgios** Feasting and folk-dancing for St. George
May 21–23 **Anastenaria** People walk on hot coals to celebrate the rescue of icons from a burning church near Thessaloníki in 1250.

Sports

Greece has a history of sports that goes back to the first Olympic Games. Boxing, running, jumping, and throwing the discus and javelin started as Olympic events then and are still part of today's Olympic Games. The 2004 Summer Games were held in Athens. More than 11,000 athletes from 201 countries competed.

Soccer and basketball are today's favorite national sports. Watersports and skiing are also very popular.

Plants

About one-fifth of Greece is covered in forest. Oak, fir, maple, and cedar trees grow in the north. Carob trees, eucalyptus, plane trees, and, above all, olive trees are also native to Greece. There are more than 6,000 species of wildflowers, including over 100 kinds of orchid.

Animals

Small numbers of bears, wolves, and lynx live in the north. Rabbits, foxes, and squirrels are common in Greece. So, too, are lizards, such as chameleons, and snakes, which include the venomous viper. There are also many species of birds, both residents and migrants.

HISTORY

People have lived throughout Greece since before the Stone Age. By 3000 B.C., people were making bronze, as well as trading in the Mediterranean region. Crete soon became the most advanced civilization in Europe.

By 800 B.C., powerful city-states were growing up. The two strongest of these, Athens and Sparta, fought each other. In the end, King Philip of Macedonia (the father of Alexander the Great) prevailed over all Greece.

In about 146 B.C., the Romans invaded. By A.D. 330, when the emperor Constantine the Great moved the capital from Rome to Constantinople (now Istanbul) in the East and became Christian, the Greeks officially became Christians, too. In time, the Romans lost control of parts of Greece to French and German knights and Venetians.

In 1453, the Turks captured most of Greece. Eventually, after nearly 400 years of Turkish rule, the Greeks won their freedom.

During World War II, the Germans and Italians occupied Greece after six months of fierce battles. Afterward, as a result of the East-West confrontation in Europe, a civil war broke out between the conservatives and the socialists-communists. The former won, and Greece joined the North Atlantic Treaty Organization (NATO).

In 1967, the army seized power in Greece. But military rule collapsed after seven years and democracy was restored.

In 1981, Greece joined the European Common Market, which is now known as the European Union.

LANGUAGE

Greek is probably the oldest European language. It was spoken as long as 4,000 years ago, and has been a written language for the past 3,000 years. The New Testament of the Bible was written in Greek. There are many words in English and other European languages that came from Greek words. The Greek alphabet has twenty-four letters. It looks different from the English alphabet. Here, English letters are used to represent Greek sounds.

Useful words and phrases

English	Greek
Zero	*mee-thén*
One	*é-na*
Two	*theé-o*
Three	*treé-a*
Four	*té-sera*
Five	*pen-de*
Six	*exi*
Seven	*ep-tá*
Eight	*och-tó*
Nine	*en-é-a*
Ten	*thé-ka*
Sunday	*ky-ri-a-ki*
Monday	*dhef-té-ra*

Useful words and phrases

English	Greek
Tuesday	*trí-ti*
Wednesday	*te-tárti*
Thursday	*pém-pti*
Friday	*pa-ra-ske-vi*
Saturday	*sá-va-to*
Hello	*kalee-mé-ra*
Good evening	*kalee-spér-ra*
Good-bye	*a-deé-o*
Please	*para-kaló*
Yes	*ne*
No	*o-hi*
Thank-you	*ef-har-ee-stó*
How are you?	*teé cán-ees?*

31

INDEX

Acknowledgments
Book created for Highlights for Children, Inc.
by Bender Richardson White.
Editors: Belinda Weber and Lionel Bender
Designer: Mike Pilley, Radius Graphics
Art Editor: Ben White
Picture Researcher: Cathy Stastny
Production: Kim Richardson

Maps produced by Oxford Cartographers, England.
Banknotes from Thomas Cook Currency Services.

Stamps courtesy of Scott Publishing Co.,
 Sidney, OH 45365 (www.scottonline.com).

Editorial Consultant: Andrew Gutelle
Greece Consultant: Loty Petrovits-Andrutsopulou
Guide to Greece is approved by the Greece National Tourist Office, London
Managing Editor, Highlights New Products: Margie Hayes Richmond

Picture credits
JD = James Davis Travel Photography. EU = Eye Ubiquitous, RH = Robert Harding Photo Library,
TL = The Travel Library, , Z = Zefa. t = top, b = bottom, l = left, r = right.
Cover: JD. Pages: 6 RH/D. Beatty. 7t: National Tourist Organization of Greece/Global Scenes, Kent. 7b: JD. 8: JD.
9t: TL/Greg Evans International. 9b: JD. 10: Life File/Oleg Svyatoslavsky. 11l: EU/Kevin Nicol. 11r: TL/Peter Terry.
12-13: Life File/Terry O'Brian. 13tl: EU/J. Waterlow. 13tr: The Complete Picture/Roger Parton. 14-15: JD.
15t: RH/G. White. 15b and 16: TL/Peter Terry. 17t: JD. 17b: EU/J. Waterlow. 18: RH/T. Gervis. 19t: Oxford
Scientific Films/William S. Paton. 19b: CORBIS/John Heseltine. 20l: CORBIS/George McCarthy. 20r and 21: RH/
David Beatty. 22-23: TL/Mike Kipling. 23t: JD. 23b: RH/G. K. Gillham. 24-25: RH/Rob Whitrow. 25t and 25b: JD.
26: RH. 27t: RH/Loraine Wilson. 27b: TL/Philip Enticknap. 28: TL/Steve Outram. 29: JD. 30: RH/Tony Gervis.
Illustration on page 1 by Tom Powers.